MY WILD LIFE
I am an OWL!

By Camilla de la Bedoyere

Miles Kelly

Look out for the 'Ask for help!' boxes. You will need help from an adult to do these activities.

Ask for help!

First published in 2012 by Miles Kelly Publishing Ltd
Harding's Barn, Bardfield End Green, Thaxted, Essex, CM6 3PX, UK
Copyright © Miles Kelly Publishing Ltd 2012

© 2012 Discovery Communications, LLC. Animal Planet and logo are trademarks of Discovery Communications, LLC, used under license. All rights reserved. www.animalplanet.co.uk

10 9 8 7 6 5 4 3 2 1

Publishing Director Belinda Gallagher
Creative Director Jo Cowan
Editorial Director Rosie McGuire
Designers Jo Cowan, Joe Jones
Image Manager Liberty Newton
Production Manager Elizabeth Collins
Reprographics Stephan Davis, Anthony Cambray, Jennifer Hunt

ISBN 978-1-84810-621-5

Printed in China

British Library Cataloguing-in-Publication Data
A catalogue record for this book is available from the British Library

ACKNOWLEDGEMENTS

The publishers would like to thank Mike Foster (Maltings Partnership), Joe Jones, and Richard Watson (Bright Agency) for the illustrations they contributed to this book.

All other artwork from the Miles Kelly Artwork Bank.

The publishers would like to thank the following sources for the use of their photographs:
t = top, b = bottom, l = left, r = right, c = centre,
bg = background, rt = repeated throughout

BOOK

Cover (front) Maksimilian/Shutterstock, (back, clockwise from bl) Miles Away Photography/Shutterstock, Kaido Karner/Shutterstock, Eric Isselée/Shutterstock

FLPA 13(b) Adri Hoogendijk/Minden Pictures; 14(tr) Mike Jones; 19(b) Erwin Van Laar/FN/Minden

Nature Picture Library 7(tr) Dietmar Nill

Photoshot 7(bl) NHPA

Shutterstock Joke panel (rt) Irzik; Heading panel (rt) PhotoDisc; Learn a Word panel (rt) Matthew Cole; 1 Eric Isselée; 2 Envita; 3 Eric Isselée; 4–5 and 5(r) Eric Isselée; 6 Kaido Karner; 8(panel, t) LittleRambo; 9(b) BooHoo, wet nose, and Lyolya; 10 Ronnie Howard; 11(t) Daniel Hebert, (b) Rick Wylie; 12–13 alarifoto; 14(bl) and 15(m) Eric Isselée, 15(tr) Ronnie Howard; 16–17(bg) Dementeva Marina&NatashaNaSt, 16(panel) yukipon, (r) Richard Laschon; 17(panel, tr) donatas1205, (tr) Dietmar Hoepfl, (cl) Solid, (cr) LittleRambo; 18–19 Lori Labrecque; 21(tl) Eric Isselée, (br) Stanislav Duben

POSTER

All images are from Shutterstock unless otherwise stated.
Martin B Withers/FLPA, David Evison, Stephen Mcsweeny, palko72, Jörn Friederich/Imagebroker/FLPA, Kaido Karner, mlorenz, Lori Labrecque, Braam Collins.

Every effort has been made to acknowledge the source and copyright holder of each picture. Miles Kelly Publishing apologizes for any unintentional errors or omissions.

Made with paper from a sustainable forest

www.mileskelly.net
info@mileskelly.net
www.factsforprojects.com

Contents

What are you?

I am an owl!

Owls are birds. We have feathers and we can fly. Our mouths are called beaks, or bills.

Hooked beak

Feathers

Q. How does a wet owl dry itself?

A. With a t-owel!

Wings

Two strong legs

Large eyes

Round face

Eurasian eagle owl
75 centimetres tall

Owl family

There are more than 200 species (types) of owl. The smallest could sit in your hand.

Sharp talons (claws)

Elf owl
12.5 centimetres tall

What do you eat?

Great grey owl

Most owls eat small animals such as mice

I eat other creatures.

My sharp talons are perfect for catching them. Animals that hunt other animals are called predators.

Tasty bugs

Some owls swoop through the air to catch insects such as crickets and moths.

Scops owl

Fish dinner

Fishing owls use their strong talons to pluck fish and frogs from the water.

Fishing owl

Knock, knock.
Who's there?
Owl.
Owl who?
Owl be seeing you!

Activity time

Get ready to make and do!

Whoo's there?

Owls have excellent hearing. How well do you and your friends hear? Take it in turns to close your eyes and listen to your friends as they each say "Twit-twoo". Can you work out who is speaking?

Feathered friends

Ask for help!

YOU WILL NEED: pinecones · felt · leaves scissors · double-sided tape · plasticine

HERE'S HOW:
1. Cut felt shapes for the owl's eyes, beak and ear tufts, and tape them in place on the pinecone.
2. Tape a leaf 'wing' to each side of the cone.
3. Add a small piece of plasticine to the bottom of the cone to help your owl stand up.

Try making lots of different owls — use buttons, feathers or shapes cut from card for the features.

Draw me!

YOU WILL NEED: pencils · paper

Now colour me in and give me a name!

1. Draw a big oval for the body and two circles for eyes.

2. Add small circles inside the eyes. Draw the beak and claws.

3. Draw a curved line on each side of the body for the wings, and add a branch.

Owl treats

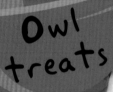

YOU WILL NEED:
· small cakes or biscuits
· white or chocolate icing
· a selection of cake decorations such as chocolate drops, silver balls, small sweets, dried fruit, chopped nuts

Ask for help!

HERE'S HOW:
Ice the tops of your cakes or biscuits. Use the decorations to create owl faces on top.

9

Where do you live?

I live in trees.

From up here I can look down on the world below me. I even perch in a tree to sleep.

Great horned owl

LEARN A WORD:
perch
The way a bird stands on a branch with its toes wrapped around it.

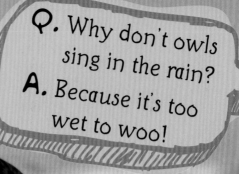

Q. Why don't owls sing in the rain?
A. Because it's too wet to woo!

Coldest owl

Snowy owls live near the North Pole where it is very cold. There are few trees, so the owls perch on the ground.

Snowy owl

Taking shelter

When it is rainy or windy, owls find a cosy hole in a tree or on the ground to sleep in. Some owls also shelter in caves and barns.

Little owl

How fast do you fly?

I fly more slowly than other hunting birds.

I spread my wings wide, and lean forwards. The wind catches my wings, and I soar through the sky.

Silent flight

Feathers soften the sound of an owl's wings. It can swoop down on a mouse before the mouse knows it is near.

Super sight

An owl's big eyes and good hearing help it to find mice moving in the grass, even when flying in the dark.

What are your babies called?

My babies are called chicks, or owlets.

Eggs and chicks

1 Chicks grow inside eggs. The eggs are almost round. They must be kept warm until they hatch.

2 The chicks have fluffy feathers to keep them warm in the nest.

Owlet

3 When it has grown its adult feathers the young owl is ready to fledge (fly away from the nest).

Fledgling

Find a nest

An owl doesn't build a nest for its eggs. It finds an old nest to lay its eggs in, or lays them in a hole in a tree.

Q. What do you call an angry owl?

A. A scowl!

15

Puzzle time

Can you solve all the puzzles?

Dinner time

Ollie the owl has to catch two mice every day to feed his chicks. How many mice does he have to catch in three days?

Wise owl

1. What type of animal is an owl – a bird or a bug?

2. Do snowy owls live in hot places or cold places?

3. What are an owl's claws called – toenails or talons?

Tell us apart

There are three differences between Oscar and Otto – can you spot them?

Oscar

Otto

Which owl?

1. I eat bugs and my name rhymes with "pops".
2. I am the smallest owl and my name rhymes with "self".
3. I make a loud noise and my name rhymes with "peach".

Catch the mouse

Can you find a way through the maze to help Olive the owl catch the mouse?

Find the answers on page 25.

What do you look like?

I am spotty and stripy.

Most owls have patterns on their feathers. They help us to hide in trees.

Screech owls

LEARN A WORD:
camouflage
Colours or patterns on an animal that help it to hide in its surroundings.

Q. What side of an owl has the most feathers?

A. The outside!

Hide and seek

Short-eared owls live in places with few trees. Their stripy feathers help camouflage them among plants on the ground.

What sound do you make?

Owls talk to each other.

Some sounds tell other owls to stay away. Others mean 'I want to meet up'. I am a barn owl and you may have heard my call.

"Twit-twoo"

Strange sound

I am a boobook owl and I am named after the noise I make!

"Boo-book"

Q. What do you call an owl with a sore throat?
A. A bird that doesn't give a hoot!

Not all owls hoot – some of them screech, hiss or whistle.

Spooky sound

I am a tawny owl and I hoot to tell other owls where I am.

"Ke-wick hoo hoo"

The Owl and the Pussycat

Use your stickers to illustrate the poem.

The Owl and the Pussy-cat went to sea
 In a beautiful pea-green boat,
They took some honey, and plenty of money,
 Wrapped up in a five-pound note.
The Owl looked up to the stars above,
 And sang to a small guitar,
"Oh, lovely Pussy, oh, Pussy, my love,
 What a beautiful Pussy you are,
  You are,
  You are!
What a beautiful Pussy
 you are!"

Pussy said to the Owl, "You elegant fowl,

How charmingly sweet you sing!

Oh, let us be married; too long we have tarried:

But what shall we do for a ring?"

They sailed away for a year and a day,

To the land where the bong-tree grows;

And there in the wood a Piggy-wig stood,

With a ring at the end of his nose,

His nose,

His nose,

With a ring at the end of his nose.

"Dear Pig, are you willing to sell for one shilling
Your ring?" Said the Piggy, "I will."
So they took it away and were married next day
By the Turkey who lives on the hill.
They dined on mince and slices of quince,
Which they ate with a runcible spoon;
And hand in hand, on the edge of the sand,
They danced by the light of the moon,
        The moon,
        The moon,
They danced by the light of the moon.

Edward Lear

24